S0-ACY-633

SandCastle

Compound Words

snow + shoe = snowshoe

Amanda Rondeau

Consulting Editor Monica Marx, M.A./Reading Specialist

Published by SandCastle™, an imprint of ABDO Publishing Company, 4940 Viking Drive, Edina, Minnesota 55435.

Printed in the United States.

Credits
Edited by: Pam Price
Curriculum Coordinator: Nancy Tuminelly
Cover and Interior Design and Production: Mighty Media
Photo Credits: Brand X Pictures, Comstock, Corbis Images, Hemera, PhotoDisc

Library of Congress Cataloging-in-Publication Data

Rondeau, Amanda, 1974-
    Snow + shoe = snowshoe / Amanda Rondeau.
      p. cm. -- (Compound words)
    Includes index.
    Summary: Illustrations and easy-to-read text introduce compound words related to snow.
    ISBN 1-59197-439-9
    1. English language--Compound words--Juvenile literature. [1. English language--Compound words.] I. Title: Snow plus shoe equals snowshoe. II. Title.

PE1175.R6679 2003
428.1--dc21

2003048120

SandCastle™ books are created by a professional team of educators, reading specialists, and content developers around five essential components that include phonemic awareness, phonics, vocabulary, text comprehension, and fluency. All books are written, reviewed, and leveled for guided reading, early intervention reading, and Accelerated Reader® programs and designed for use in shared, guided, and independent reading and writing activities to support a balanced approach to literacy instruction.

Let Us Know

After reading the book, SandCastle would like you to tell us your stories about reading. What is your favorite page? Was there something hard that you needed help with? Share the ups and downs of learning to read. We want to hear from you! To get posted on the ABDO Publishing Company Web site, send us e-mail at:

sandcastle@abdopub.com

SandCastle Level: Transitional

34487081 10/06

A compound word is two words joined together to make a new word.

snow + shoe =

snowshoe

The Smith family likes to snowshoe in the winter.

snow + suit =

snowsuit

Bill likes to play in the snow.

He stays warm in his snowsuit.

snow + ball =

snowball

It is fun to make a big snowball and see how far you can throw it.

snow + storm =

snowstorm

The Green family plays outside after a snowstorm.

The snow is soft and fluffy.

snow + man =

snowman

Amy put a hat and a scarf on the snowman.

chair + lift =

chairlift

Mark and his family
ride the chairlift
when they ski.

Mary and the Snowman

After the snowstorm
little Mary the mouse
built a snowman that
was as big as a house.

The snowman threw snowballs
that landed very near.

Mary walked in her snowshoes
right up to his ear.

"Hey, snowman," she said.
"Don't throw snowballs at me!"

So Mary and the snowman went to his icehouse and drank some tea.

More Compound Words

bobsled	snowflake
broomball	snowmelt
dogsled	snowmobile
downhill	snowplow
outerwear	sweatshirt
snowboard	turtleneck
snowdrift	underwear

Glossary

chairlift   chairs that hang from a cable and carry people to the top of a mountain

icehouse   a building where ice is made, stored, or sold

snowshoes   webbed devices worn on the feet to keep them from sinking into deep snow

snowstorm   a winter storm with heavy snowfall

snowsuit   a suit worn by children in the winter to keep them warm

About SandCastle™

A professional team of educators, reading specialists, and content developers created the SandCastle™ series to support young readers as they develop reading skills and strategies and increase their general knowledge. The SandCastle™ series has four levels that correspond to early literacy development in young children. The levels are provided to help teachers and parents select the appropriate books for young readers.

Emerging Readers
(no flags)

Beginning Readers
(1 flag)

Transitional Readers
(2 flags)

Fluent Readers
(3 flags)

These levels are meant only as a guide. All levels are subject to change.

To see a complete list of SandCastle™ books and other nonfiction titles from ABDO Publishing Company, visit www.abdopub.com or contact us at:

4940 Viking Drive, Edina, Minnesota 55435 • 1-800-800-1312 • fax: 1-952-831-1632